Star of HIGH SCHOOL MUSICAL

and more!

ASHLEY TISDALE

POSY EDWARDS

ashley tisdale

FULL NAME: Ashley Michelle Tisdale

BIRTHDAY: 2 July 1985

BIRTHPLACE: West Deal, New Jersey

HEIGHT: 5′ 3″

NICKNAME: Pookernuts

EYES: Brown

HOME: Valencia, California

STAR SIGN: Cancer

SHE CAN'T LIVE WITHOUT: Peanut butter Cap n' Crunch and vanilla ice blend from Coffee Bean.

BROTHERS AND SISTERS: Parents are Lisa and Mike Tisdale and elder sister is actress Jennifer Tisdale.

PETS: A dog named Blondie, which is also her nickname on The Suite Life of Zack & Cody.

FAMOUS RELATIVES: Her grandfather, Arnold Morris, made Ginsu knives popular in the US, plus her cousin, Ron Popeil, is an inventor.

FAVOURITE COLOUR: Pink, of course!

FAVORITE MOVIES: Peter Pan, Just Married, My Best Friend's Wedding, and How to Lose a Guy in 10 Days.

FAVOURITE SPORT: Basketball, it's the only one she can slightly understand!

HIDDEN TALENT: Horseback riding

FAVOURITE BOOK: The Great Gatsby by F. Scott Fitzgerald

FAVOURITE CAR: Range Rover

FAVOURITE HSM SONG: 'Breaking Free'

BEST FRIENDS (APART FROM HER BIG SIS, OF COURSE): Brittany Snow and Vanessa Hudgens.

FAVOURITE SHOP: Hollister

FAVOURITE TV SHOW: Friends

FAVOURITE CLOTHES: Diesel, Bebe, Urban Outfitters and Forever 21.

MOST PRIZED POSSESSION: Her new Louis Vuitton bag.

HAIR: Naturally dark brown. She dyed it blonde upon landing the part of Maddie Fitzpatrick.

FAVOURITE ACTORS: Brittany Murphy, Julia Roberts, Johnny Depp and Leonardo DiCaprio.

FAVORITE MUSIC: Billy Joel, Elton John, Mariah Carey, The Used, All American Rejects, and Nick Lachey.

FAVOURITE FOOD: Sushi

5

O.M.G! It sure has been a crazy few years for young Ashley Tisdale!

From being spotted in a shopping mall aged just three years old, to rocketing to the top of Tinseltown's 'Most Wanted' list, Ashley's rise has been a Hollywood phenomenon. The all-American blonde bombshell can do it all! You name it, be it singing on Broadway or in front of the President, breaking chart records or simply starring in the most successful musical trilogy of all time.

It makes you wonder what's left for her to do. At this rate, she's on course to being the most revered blonde in Hollywood since Marilyn Monroe, and no doubt she'll be singing and dancing all the way there! Not only has Ashley Tisdale arrived folks, she's going to be around and at the top for a long time to come…

A Star is born!

On 2 July 1985, the big brown eyes of newborn baby girl Ashley Tisdale first opened onto the world. When her beaming parents, Mike and Lisa, brought her back to the Tisdale family home in West Deal, New Jersey, they just knew they were holding a future star in their arms. Ashley's devilishly cheeky smile and playful wit were hallmarks of a childhood that was full of happy times.

ASH FACT!

Ashley's not the only star in her family. Her big sister, Jennifer, is also an actress, who's most known for starring in hit film Bring It On: In It To Win It

ASH FACT!
Ashley's star sign is Cancer meaning she is loving and sympathetic but can get moody on her bad days!

Home sweet home

Growing up in a white picket-fenced community, Ashley had a typical all-American upbringing. Her summer days were spent running around the wild countryside on family days out, while in the winter she'd snuggle up at home with her pals and gossip about boys. But nothing was, or is, more important to Ashley than her family. Ashley claims that the most important person in the world to her is 'My mom. She has helped me get where I am today. She is my support and my best friend. I love her.'

Ashley's one in a thousand

Picture the scene: it's 1988 in a typical suburban American shopping mall and talent scout Bill Perlman is holding auditions to try to discover the next Madonna or Michael Jackson. Needless to say, every single wannabe in the entire state came flocking to the auditions and the queue extended for miles. Sadly for the talent scout, none of the hopefuls seemed to have the magical 'x-factor' he was looking for. But whilst on a break from the endless line of auditions, Bill spotted three year-old Ashley walking through the mall with her mother. According to him, 'She had a head full of beautiful curly hair, huge eyes, and when she looked at me, she made the hugest of smiles. I followed her into the store and asked if they were going to be participating in the talent show. I was told, "not interested, but thanks." I left them to their shopping, knowing with certainty that

they had no idea what I could do for them or what she was missing.'

Bill Perlman was so adamant that Ashley was a future star, he tracked down the mother and daughter in the mall later that day and insisted on giving Ashley's mother his business card. Who knows where Ash would be today without that chance encounter!

Model, actress, singer!

A few months later Ashley's mother gave Bill Perlman a call. It wasn't long before Ashley was at her first casting. Needless to say, the beautiful brown-eyed Ashley was snapped up! Her first job was modelling clothes for JC Penney. For the promising three year-old it was to be the first success of many. Over the coming years the bright young starlet appeared in over 100 television commercials, the most famous of which included a T-Mobile ad with none other than Catherine Zeta-Jones! According to Ashley, 'it was the best experience. For four days I went to Canada and got to work with Catherine Zeta-Jones! She's so nice. It was so much fun!'

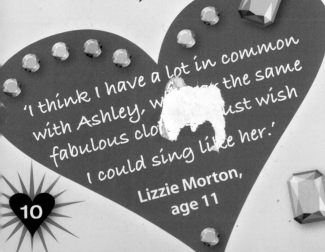

'I think I have a lot in common with Ashley, we like the same fabulous clo... I just wish I could sing like her.'

Lizzie Morton, age 11

10

show time

Broadway star

After quite a long period of doing commercials, Ashley began to tire of doing the same repetitive work. Occasionally, the Tisdale family would drive the two hours up the freeway to New York in order to catch a show on Broadway. On one of these trips they watched *Les Misérables*, Ashley fell in love with the performance and made it her next goal to land a part in the stage show. Ever successful, Ashley was stepping out on Broadway within months! 'When I was little, I saw the play *Les Misérables* on Broadway. I thought it was the most amazing thing I had ever seen. So I went to my manager and told him I wanted to be in it. He asked me if I could sing, and I said no. He said, "You have to be able to sing in *Les Misérables*." ' So,

'Ashley rocks the screen every time! I love her!'

Cat Lyons, age 9

Ashley tottered off and had herself just one singing lesson before auditioning for the part of Cossette, which she of course landed with ease!

Ashley then went on tour with *Les Mis* for 18 months. At the age of eight that's a very long time to be away from home. Not only did she have to learn her lines, she had to keep her voice in tip-top shape to be able to perform every day. But ever positive, Ashley maintains that the whole experience of touring with the world's most successful musical 'was amazing. I think it helped me get to the place where I am today. It taught me discipline and helped me get over being shy.'

Ashley takes centre stage

After the phenomenal success of starring in *Les Misérables*, it was inevitable that other Broadway casting directors would come knocking for the latest child prodigy to hit the famous Manhattan musical scene. Ashley was soon starring in the title role of *Annie* and singing well known classics such as *It's a Hard Knock Life* and *Tomorrow*. Again Ashley had reached a major milestone in her still very young career.

Mr President

During her fantastically successful Broadway years, Ashley got called to sing at the White House for President Clinton! Needless to say this is still one of the proudest moments of the all-American gal's life: 'I was part of Broadway Kids, which was a bunch of kids who were in Broadway shows, and we sang Broadway tunes and met the president,' says Ashley. 'I was so nervous but it was really fun.'

ASH FACT!
The Broadway role of Annie had previously been occupied by Hollywood heavyweight Sarah Jessica Parker, an idol of Ashley's!

don't go changin'

Despite Ashley's great desire to pursue her Hollywood and Broadway dreams of acting, her family were adamant that she shouldn't get carried away with herself: 'I always had a normal life,' Ashley explains. My dad wanted me to know how long it took to make money and not to take anything for granted.' And the same applied for Ashley's school career. Sure, Ashley would while away her weekends in the mall with her pals – but not unless her homework was done first. She also had the continual lure of her dreams of stardom pulling her. Luckily for Ashley her father was there to set her straight: 'My dad is adamant about education,' Ashley says.

ASH FACT!

Before she made millions as a top actress and singer, Ashley made ends meet by working in clothes stores: 'It wasn't fun,' she says. 'But I did love getting a discount.'

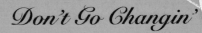

Bookworm

Outside of drama, and in the classroom, Ashley was quite the studious swot: 'My favourite subject was English or creative writing,' she says. 'We did poems and made a magazine and I did one on celebrities. I called it *Celebrity Life Magazine*.' Little did she think she'd be on the pages of star magazines herself just a few years later!

Cheerleading rocks!

Ashley's elder sister Jennifer encouraged the shy Ashley to get into cheerleading to try and give her baby sister more confidence: 'My sister was a hard-core cheerleader and I always wanted to follow her,' says Ashley. 'I was really shy when I was younger and cheerleading helped me come out of my shell.' Whooping and hollering in front of her school football team and all the fans opened Ashley up, and once she realised she had a true inner performer there was no stopping her!

a girl's best friend

Ashley and Sharpay agree that no girl should be without a dog – they are just the cutest things! Not only are they fun and cute, but they are becoming the ultimate Hollywood accessory. Which one would you choose?

1. Pick your favourite pooch!

2. Pick a perfect doggie-sized bag!

3. Now, for the accessories!

Here's Sharpay's favourite pup – why not accessorise it to match your style!

YOU WILL NEED:
glue, coloured pens, scissors, glitter, sheets of colour paper (lots of pink, obviously). If you don't have coloured paper – use white and colour it in

And now you're ready to start accessorising! Cut out lots of different accessories from the pieces of paper (glittery bows, adorable doggy jackets, cute bonnets – whatever you need to make your dog look glam) and using your glue, stick them on to Ashley's yorkie! And don't forget to customise your own dog tag – lots of glitter, hearts, pink and your name essential!

lights, camera action!

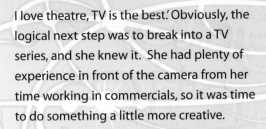

So, before even hitting her teens, Ashley had achieved more than most actors and actresses would in a lifetime. She was the hottest child star on Broadway, and had over 100 commercials to prove it. But Ashley wanted to spread her wings and try new things. While the advertising work paid her big bucks, Ashley wanted to be more creative, and when it came to Broadway and the theatre Ashley says that 'actually, I prefer TV. Even though I love theatre, TV is the best.' Obviously, the logical next step was to break into a TV series, and she knew it. She had plenty of experience in front of the camera from her time working in commercials, so it was time to do something a little more creative.

From stage to screen

Ashley hit the TV auditions circuit and quickly realised what a tough world being an actress can be. For a while rejection followed rejection, as casting directors seemed to always be looking for a girl who was shorter, taller, fatter, thinner, blonder or more brunette. But Ashley refused to take anything personally and just kept turning up at auditions with that fabulous smile on her face. After a while her diligence paid off and she landed parts in a couple of trial shows. Unfortunately, the shows weren't successful and the shows were never made – more frustration for young Ashley.

But, Ashley being Ashley, success was only around the corner. Aged just 12, she finally made it onto her first TV show, *Smart Guy* – a show about a super-genius kid trying to fit into normal life. Ashley was in an episode named 'Knowledge College' and soon after she landed another small role in *7th Heaven*, a show about an American priest and his family.

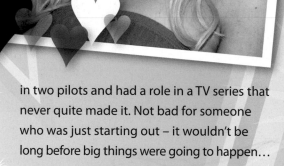

Lights, Camera, Action!

After this little run of success, Ashley thought she'd cracked the TV business. Sadly she was to learn what a fickle business showbiz is. It took three whole years of auditions before she was to land another TV role. During this period, she knuckled down at school, but still kept turning up to audition after audition and giving it one hundred percent. That's Ashley!

Out from the shadows

In early 2000, Ashley finally saw some results for all her persistence. She got to play a cameo role in the cult-hit show, *Beverley Hills 90210*! After doing such a good job in that the offers to do guest appearances came streaming in. *Boston Public, Malcolm in the Middle* and *Charmed* are just a few of the shows she starred in. It wasn't long before Ashley landed her first regular slot. *Nathan's Choice* was a novel sitcom about the ups and downs of a recent graduate. The show allowed viewers to decide on the plot by voting for various storylines online or by phone. Ashley had landed the part of Stephanie, and was super-psyched to be playing her first regular role. Unfortunately, the show wasn't a success and it was cancelled before it had a chance to air.

So, more let downs for Ashley, but in a very short period of time Ashley had built up a very impressive CV, having made 21 guest appearances in 16 shows, plus she'd starred in two pilots and had a role in a TV series that never quite made it. Not bad for someone who was just starting out – it wouldn't be long before big things were going to happen…

Ashley hits the big screen

She was becoming such a well-known name among casting directors in Hollywood that it's no surprise that the film industry wanted to work with her. *Donnie Darko* was the cult hit of 2001. Ashley only played the small role of dorky girl, Kim, but the film was a huge success both at the box office and with the critics. Not to mention that fact that Ashley got to meet Hollywood heartthrob, Jake Gyllenhaal, who played the lead role in the film. What more could a girl wish for?

ASH FACT!

Who's Ashley biggest celebrity crush? 'I'd have to say Jake Gyllenhaal. I worked with him in Donnie Darko, so that was really cool,' says Ashley.

23

Suite Life

24

Ashley's big break

Ashley's name was now well-known amongst all the agents and casting directors on the kids TV circuit. So when Disney put together the idea for a show based around the life of twins who grow up in a swanky hotel to be named *The Suite Life of Zack & Cody*, they knew that they had to get Ashley involved.

So Maddie or London?

But for which part would they choose Ashley? While the directors were certain they wanted the talented teenager to be involved in the programme, they couldn't decide on which role they wanted her to play: Maddie

ASH FACT!

The Suite Life of Zack & Cody *is filmed in the same studio as* That's So Raven *and* Hannah Montana.

or London? The two roles couldn't be more different. London, who is the spoiled self-centred daughter of the hotel owner, is the polar opposite of Maddie, the lovely angelic girl who runs the candy counter. It's a true testament to Ashley's versatility as an actress that she was considered ideal for either role. Later in her career, it came as no great surprise to the *Suite Life* directors that she turned her hand so easily to playing the role of Sharpay in *High School Musical*.

In the end, the directors chose her to play the role of Maddie, much to the delight of Ashley, who was keen to play a more likeable role in the early stages of her career: 'I'm really glad that I ended up with Maddie,' says Ashley. 'Because for fans to get to know me, I'd rather them look up to this character, who is more like me rather than Sharpay.'

Now that Ashley had been accepted into the Disney family, she'd be working in the same studios as her idols – Hilary Swank, Justin Timberlake and Britney Spears – had done in the formative years of their careers.

the suite life co-stars

Cole and Dylan Sprouse

The gorgeous blonde twins were born in Arezzo, Italy (where their American parents were teaching English) on 4 August 1992. Dylan, the elder by 15 minutes, was named after the poet Dylan Thomas, while Cole was named after Nat King Cole. Shortly after the birth of the twins the Sprouse family moved back to California and the twins started their acting career aged only six months! Being identical they often shared a role and played the part of Patrick Kelly in *Grace Under Fire* for the first five years of their life. Talk about experience from a young age!

Their big break came when they played opposite Adam Sandler in *Big Daddy*, of which Ashley says: 'When *Big Daddy* came out, I fell in love with the boys and told my mom I was going to work with them some day.

When I found out they were in* The Suite Life, *I freaked out and said, "I have to get this job!" Which of course she did!

They now play in their most famous role, as the mischievous twins Zack and Cody. The roles were based around the twins' actual personalities; Dylan plays Zack,

and much like his character he's the more boisterous, cheeky and mischievous one. Cole, who plays Cody, is a little quieter and more innocent.

The twins have also appeared in episodes of *That 70's Show* and *Nightmare Room* and have even broken out from their pairing and worked individually, most notably when Cole played the role of Ben Geller (Ross's son) in *Friends*.

Sprouse Brother Facts

BORN: Arezzo, Italy on 4 August 1992

PETS: Two dogs named Bubba and Currey

HOBBIES: Skateboarding, surfing, snowboarding, motocross and basketball

SCHOOL SUBJECTS: Dylan likes history; Cole likes maths and science

FAVOURITE FILM: Dylan likes *Napoleon Dynamite*; Cole likes *Forrest Gump* and *Godzilla*

FAVOURITE COMPUTER GAME: Dylan likes *Super Smash Bros*; Cole likes *Legend of Zelda*

Brenda Song

*I*n *The Suite Life* beautiful Brenda plays the mean and spiteful role of London Tipton, but she's been on the teen-star circuit for years, having played major roles in films such as *Get a Clue, Like Mike* and, of course, the huge Disney success, *Wendy Wu: Homecoming Warrior.* Obviously, she's nothing like the foot-stomping little madam London Tipton in real life, but she certainly loves the role: 'It's so much fun to play London,' Brenda says, 'because she's my fantasy character. Her daddy owns the hotel, she shops until she drops, everyone works for her, and her closet is a dream.' Also, unlike her character, she loves the people she works with, in particular the twins.

Brenda on the Sprouse Brothers:
'The Sprouse twins are like my brothers.'

Brenda says 'I love them so much. They are so intelligent and genuine. They're crazy game loving 12-year-old boys.' But would they ever dare pull the crazy pranks that their troublesome characters ever play in the show? 'They know better than to mess with the queen of pranks,' says Brenda.

As for Ashley and Brenda, despite their two characters on the show being very different, in real life 'Brenda and I are like sisters,' says Ashley. 'On our lunch breaks we go shopping and get our nails done. I knew Brenda for four years before the show even started.'

Ashley says: 'It's the coolest thing to get to work with my best friend.'

Brenda Song Facts

BORN: 27 March 1988 in Carmichael, California.

FAVOURITE FOOD: Mexican

FAVOURITE MUSIC: Eminem and Avril Lavigne

FASHION ICON: Jennifer Lopez

HIDDEN TALENT: Brenda has a black belt in tae kwon do – You go girl!

The sweet life on Suite Life...

*T*hriving in her first regular role on a major TV series, Ashley threw herself into the role of Maddie, and worked her socks off with the rest of the cast.

'Everyone's a huge family. It's great to get to work with people you love.'

She also adores her character but says that 'she is not like me. I love her style. She is a little bit more sarcastic than I am. She's a funny girl and always getting into trouble with London, but she always knows how to get out of it; she's a really smart girl and I love portraying someone who is really smart.'

Suite future

*T*he hugely successful Disney show has run for three full series and will continue with the spin-off show *Suite Life on Deck*. Unfortunately, Ashley won't continue to work on the new programme but she is rumoured to appear in a few episodes as a guest star. The exciting new show is due to be aired on Disney sometime this year. Even though Ashley will be missing, it should be a very exciting new programme, with lots of familiar faces. Brenda Song and the twins, Dylan and Cody Sprouse, are definitely going to be in the new cast, with some new exciting stars promised.

ASH FACT!

Ashley's favourite episode of Suite Life... is 'Rockstar in the House' starring super-hunk Jesse McCartney. Ashley says 'he is so cute. It was such a great episode and so much fun to do. It was really cool and a great experience working with Jesse.'

high school musical

Landing the dream role

Not long after Ashley had got stuck into her role as Maddie in *Suite Life*, rumours started spreading around Hollywood that Disney was casting for a new teenage musical. Ashley had grown up watching movies such as *Grease*, *West Side Story* and *Dirty Dancing*, so when she heard that Kenny Ortega (choreographer of *Dirty Dancing* and *Ferris Bueller's Day Off*) was onboard she knew she had to get in the film.

In their search for new faces, the producers sent out an open casting call, meaning that literally anyone could turn up and try out. Hordes of wannabes descended on the Disney studios from all over the US in hope of being the next teen sensation. Fortunately, the producer Billy Borden already knew of her: 'I didn't know any of these kids, except for Ashley Tisdale,' says Billy. 'I knew her from the Disney show (*The Suite Life of Zack & Cody*).' So Ashley's career to date already gave her a head start over the other kids at the auditions, but her previous work with Disney didn't mean she was given special preference. Ashley says that her starring role in the film 'wasn't given to me. A lot of people think it is because I'm on Disney, but I had to go on the audition, and to the call-back. It wasn't like it was handed to me at all. I had to go in there and get it myself.'

★SHARPAY★

Not Sharpay!

Naturally, being Ashley, she sparkled in all the auditions and stood out as one of the top female performers. Her role as Maddie in *Suite Life* meant that she'd have no problems at all playing the good-as-gold lead character of Gabriella, but again her versatility shone through and the producers decided to cast her as the conniving and vain Sharpay. Ashley was delighted with her new role as it meant she'd be able to spread her wings and add more characteristics to her dramatic range. After all, playing different roles such as Maddie and Sharpay is why Ashley has always loved acting so much in the first place: 'I get to be all different characters that tell different stories,' Ashley says.

'Maddie and Sharpay are totally different.'

'Maddie's, like, this girl next door, she's really sweet, and Sharpay is just the total opposite. She's the most popular girl. She dresses like she's going to a red-carpet event. It's funny because she's mean, but she always has a smile on. But they're totally different.'

'I love the way Ashley can play all sorts of characters. She can do anything!'
Claire Simons, age 10

Getting into character

Now that she'd landed the major role of playing East High's queen diva, she had to work on being catty and scheming, but it didn't come naturally to sweet-natured Ashley. In order to ready herself she drew on other films for inspiration: 'I watched a lot of movies to prepare for playing her,' says Ashley. 'I actually watched *Mean Girls*, with Rachel McAdams, and I liked how she portrayed her character. She was a mean girl, but she had a smile on her face whenever she did it. So I watched all these other things and kind of put in some things and made it creative myself. I just loved playing the mean girl.'

ASH FACT!
Ashley's least favourite scene in HSM was when she got chilli dumped on her. 'It was horrible. It smelled so bad!'

Practice, practice, practice!

It was a hard slog for Ashley and the gang from the very start. Disney, not expecting a massive success, had allocated the tiny (in Hollywood terms) budget of $5million. So time and money were short. The cast had to get up to speed, and quick. Zac says of the first day's rehearsals: 'We didn't know what we were doing, we were thrown into this dance room and there were mirrors everywhere! We didn't know anything about each other and had to learn these dances.'

It ain't easy at the top!

For two weeks Ashley and the main cast were putting in 12-hour days, mastering dance moves and basketball skills. 'We had two weeks of intense dancing, acting, singing, and basketball rehearsals along with strange stretching [exercises] and things I'd never heard of before,' says Zac. 'We'd wake up at six in the morning and work until six at night. It was a very long day – by the end I'd sustained so many injuries and was so sore but so much better than I was before. I learned more in those two weeks than I'd learned in the previous

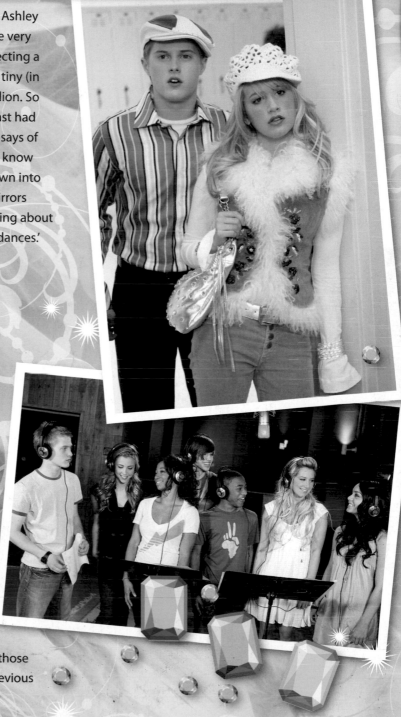

years. Every second of it was worth it. At the end of the day, I just remember being so beat and beyond tired. I reached a new level of sleep every night. It was crazy.'

Practice makes perfect!

By the time it came to shooting the film, Ashley and the rest of the cast aced it. The evidence is there for all to see in the movie. Even while filming it they knew they were creating something special and unique. 'There were moments, there were little glimmers shooting a couple of scenes that there's something special going here, specifically the final scene' says Monique Coleman, who stars as Taylor.

Ashley forged a lifelong bond with the cast and crew. Having that many like-minded kids together made a special summer that Ashley would never forget. Luckily she'd get to do it all again. Twice!

ASH FACT!
One of the hardest things Ashley had to get used to while playing Sharpay was wearing heels! 'I never really liked high heels and I was really scared because she wore heels all the time.'

HSM co-stars

Best friend Vanessa Hudgens

*D*espite constantly being at odds on screen, Vanessa (also known as one half of the super-couple, Zanessa) and Ashley are totally BFF off-screen. Born in California, Vanessa has been singing and dancing to musicals for years. Just like Ashley, Vanessa first went on stage at a young age, treading the boards for the first time when she was only eight! Her first film was *Thirteen* and she also worked with Disney on *Thunderbirds*. She's known best friend Ashley ever since doing a commercial together years ago, Vanessa says 'my best friend is actually Ashley Tisdale!'

'After we knew we had gotten High School Musical *we just ran up and jumped up and down like a pair of little girls. We were so excited!'*

They've also worked together on *The Suite Life of Zack and Cody*, which goes someway to explaining their ease with each other on camera. Much like the others, however, it was *High School Musical* that shot Vanessa to fame. Her role as Gabriella Montez has won her and Zac the 'Best Chemistry' award at the Teenchoice Awards in 2006. Soon after

Vanessa Facts

BORN: 14 December, 1988 in Salinas, California

FAVOURITE HOBBY: Shopping, of course!

GUILTY PLEASURE: 'Any kind of chocolate, I will eat it. I've always loved it ever since I was little. I even have it by my bedside.'

FAVOURITE CARTOON: Spongebob Squarepants

HSM Co-stars

the smash hit film, she signed to Hollywood Records, with whom she has released 'Come Back To Me' and 'Say OK.'

Girls rock!

Vanessa says, 'I want to put like a new genre together. Kind of soulful and kind of rock, and just different, very eclectic. I definitely want to do my thing.' With more albums in the pipeline, 2009's release of *Will* – her first lead in a feature film – and being part of the hottest relationship since 'Brangelina,' it looks like we'll be seeing much more of Vanessa's pretty face in the coming years!

Zac Facts

BORN: 18 October, 1987 in San Luis Obispo, California

HIDDEN TALENTS: 'I can blow bubbles with my spit.' Gross!

FAVOURITE BOOKS: *Busting Vegas* by Ben Mezrich and *Robinson Crusoe* by Daniel Defoe

FAVOURITE BAND: The Postal Service

FAVOURITE MOVIE: *The Goonies*

The gorgeous Zac Efron

The hunky blue-eyed babe, and star of the show, had been knocking around the child actors scene for years before *HSM*. He first became well-known to us when he played the sultry surfer dude, Cameron Bale, in *Summerland*. But it was landing the role of high school super-jock, Troy, that sent Zac to the top of Hollywood's A-list. Days before flying out to the set of *HSM*, Ashley heard that not only would she be working with her old friend, Zac, but she'd also be flying out to the set with him too! Of course, she immediately rang him to say they were flying out from LA together. Ashley had known Zac for a couple of years from the child actors' LA circuit, and was totally stoked to have a friend from the beginning on such a large and daunting project.

Since *HSM*'s phenomenal success, Zac has gone on to great things, starring in *Hairspray* with his idol John Travolta, and high school comedy, *Seventeen*. The kid's got all of Hollywood at his feet and is set to reach the top. Good job he'll have his good pal, Ashley, around to ensure he keeps his feet on the ground!

ASH FACT!

In Ashton Kutcher's MTV show Punk'd, Ashton pranks Zac when he is accused of helping a thief steal some money from a Rodeo Drive boutique. Guess who was behind the prank? Zac's friend Ashley, of course!

Cool Corbin Bleu

Wild haired Corbin plays Chad Danforth, Troy's best bud and fellow hottie. Corbin reckons him and his character have similarities and differences. 'Chad is a very passionate person about everything he does, which is something we have in common' Corbin says, 'Where we are not alike is that Chad is not open to new things. I love change.'

No stranger to performing, Corbin has literally been in front of cameras all his life, having been in commercials as a baby, so acting in films never gets him nervous. It's singing that gives him the jitters! Before recording 'I get so nervous I can't sing,' he says. 'I freak out when I hear my own voice.'

He must have gotten over it because his new album, *Another Side*, was released in 2007.

He says that if he could perform with anyone it would be Beyoncé. At the rate his career's escalating, she'll be lucky! Beyoncé and Corbin? Watch this space…

Magic Monique Coleman

Monique, who plays Taylor Mckessie, is one of the older members of the cast, so coming into filming she had quite a bit of experience and maturity over the others. Over the years she's done quite a bit of TV work and had worked with Ashley before on *The Suite Life of Zack and Cody*. She's also been in hits shows such as *Malcolm in the Middle*, *Gilmore Girls*, *Boston Public* and *Veronica Mars*. She loved playing the role of Taylor but admits there were differences between herself and her character: 'My character is a little bit brighter in the math and science department than I am … okay, a lot!' Working on *HSM* has been Monique's largest project, but beyond the success, it's the friendships and family environment the cast have made that have been one of the biggest bonuses for her.

'We are really like family, and I really get along with everyone. We see a lot of one another.'

Monique
Facts

BORN: November 13, 1980 in Orangeburg, South Carolina.

FAVOURITE MUSICAL: *Fame*

FAVOURITE BAND: Black Eyed Peas.

FAVOURITE HOBBY: camping.

LIFE GOAL: to be a source of inspiration to others.

41

Lucas Facts

BORN: 24 November, 1984 in Springfield Missouri

FAVOURITE ANIMATED FILM: *The Fox and the Hound*

HIDDEN TALENT: he plays both the drums and the guitar

A FAVOURITE GOLDEN OLDIE FILM: *Singin' in the Rain*

PETS: a Maltese poodle called Lilly

Cute Lucas Grabeel

"I'm like Ryan because I have a strong background in theatre and I did a lot of performing while growing up."

ucas moved to LA to find fame and fortune when he was 18 and for a while he worked in a video store to help support his career. In a bizarre stroke of luck, Lucas met his agent randomly one day while queuing for a smoothie in a mall. Within weeks he was shooting Disney's *Halloweentown High*. Since doing *High School Musical*, he's landed a guest starring role in *Boston Legal* and a recurring role on UPN's *Veronica Mars*.

Lucas reckons his success is down to 'setting goals early in life, always believing that if it can be dreamed, it can be reached.' But thankfully Hollywood hasn't changed him too much and he's kept his feet on the ground: 'I am a simple plain person. You know?' Lucas says. 'I'm chilled and laid back and not so out there and crazy.'

ASH FACT!

Ashley is the first ever female artist to have two singles debut at the same time in the US top 100 chart.

reach for the stars!

*A*fter all the hard work of dancing, singing and acting, by the time *HSM*'s opening night came around Ashley was exhausted. So on 20 January 2006, Ashley and her family gathered around the living room to watch the premiere of *High School Musical*. Disney had been advertising the show over the Christmas period, and hype and excitement had been building in the Tisdale household!

Next stop ... global superstar!

*W*hat Ashley or anyone else hadn't realised was that a similar buzz was growing in homes across the States. 7.7 million viewers tuned in that evening, smashing Disney's viewing records! Disney went on to air the show eleven more times totalling an audience of 36 million viewers. That's a lot of people!

Within weeks Ashley and the gang were

in every teeny magazine. Crowds were mobbing her wherever she went. It was the success story of 2006, and it was only January! It wasn't long before the Disney execs were sending the film abroad to be viewed in homes across the globe. At the time, no one was prepared for the emphatic reception *High School Musical* received, but Ashley felt the main reason for its success was down to how easy it was for the kids to be able to relate to the show: 'I think these characters are really relatable,' Ash says. 'You've gone to school with our characters. I think they're a little bit exaggerated. But, you know, everyone has a Sharpay and everyone has a brainy girl. It's actually, like, you relate to it, especially adults do.'

But beyond all the records Ashley is super proud of the message the film sends out. 'The whole movie is about being true to yourself and not being in a clique,' she says. 'You don't have to be just one thing. Kids can get stuck in a clique and can't get out of it. You feel that people won't support you in anything else. I think it's important to find yourself in school and be happy about it.'

In the spotlight

Despite being relatively well known from *The Suite Life of Zack & Cody*, nothing had prepared Ashley for the galactic stardom *HSM* would send her and the leading cast into: 'It's crazy. It's, like, it's huge!' Ash says. 'I mean we never expected this much. We knew the movie was going to be really good because we can feel that. And we knew it was going to be fun, and kids would like it. It's really, really awesome!' At last Ashley had arrived into the big time, and she's here to stay!

Chart topper

As well as breaking all the television records, *HSM*'s soundtrack was dominating the charts. Most of the plaudits were going to Vanessa and Zac, but Ashley's songs 'What I've Been Looking For', 'Bop to the Top', and 'We're All in This Together', all jumped to the top end of the charts, much to the surprise of Ashley: 'I think the album coming out of leftfield and going gold is, like, absolutely nuts. We never imagined that in a million years.'

ASH FACT!

Ashley thinks the most important part of friendship is showing support: 'If people don't support you, they're not your real friends.'

46

the look

Ashley stylin'

Now that Ashley is on top of the world, she's one of the most revered style icons for girls all over, but she's got idols of her own – in particular Jessica Simpson: 'I would take a picture with Jessica Simpson because I love her style.' But how does she create her effortless style?

So, Sharpay or Maddie?

Depending on her mood Ashley takes on the style of her various characters. When she's going to the mall with Vanessa or hanging out at home she dresses more like Maddie who is 'very casual and comfy,' says Ash. But when Ashley is hitting the red carpet she takes from Sharpay's sparkling wardrobe, although she admits her HSM character can be a little extreme: 'Sharpay was way over the top and bedazzled. Her style was based on my cell phone, which is pink and sparkly. I'm a mix of both because I love to wear Uggs and leggings and be casual, but I also like dressing up!'

Ashley's Top Style Tips

⭐ **Clothes, hair and make-up** Get your order right and start with the clothes: 'I always pick my wardrobe first. Once I have that, I do my hair and then match my makeup.'

⭐ **Look after your luscious locks** Look after your hair, especially if you want to keep it straight like Ashley's: 'Deep conditioning is essential because I have naturally curly hair and straighten it a lot – otherwise it's going to die.'

⭐ **Glamour on a budget** You don't need expensive and flashy clothes to be stylish: 'I like to wear sweats and cute T-shirts. Sometimes if I'm going out, I'll wear jeans and a cute top.'

⭐ **Shoes glorious shoes!** When it comes to shoes, choose comfort over style: 'I'm horrible in heels. I have to wear flats. I have the cutest ballerina slippers for dressy events.'

⭐ **Customise!** Don't be afraid to experiment: 'Lately, I've been wearing pinstriped shorts over leggings and I just bought a wide belt that comes up under my chest.'

CREATE YOUR OWN ASHLEY STYLE!

Your stage name...

Favourite colour..

Favourite dog...

Hair colour...

Hair up or down?..

Eye colour..

Style – Maddie or Sharpay?......................................

Lip gloss – pink, red or clear?.................................

Accessories – bag, belt, sunglasses?

....

Dress or jeans and a top?

....

Heels or flats?...

ASH FACT!
Despite being the beautiful blonde bombshell she is today, Ashley wasn't always a style icon. 'At high school I was really dorky' she says.

Ashley wouldn't go out of the house without:
Her favourite pink lip gloss

A pair of ballet pumps for when her feet get sore!

Her handbag – every girl needs one

Her sparkly cell phone

Her dog Blondie of course!

WHAT WOULD BE ON YOUR LIST?

Be the superstar you are!

What you'll need in your make up bag:

Eye shadows – classic browns and golds, and as many of your favourite colours as you want!

Mascara – brown or black

Blusher – pink or peach

Lip gloss – pink, red or clear

Shimmer dust – for extra sparkle!

Get the look

★ Sharpay really knows how to make the most of her beautiful brown eyes and here's how she does it: Use light, medium and dark eyeshadow shades in graduated tones (shades of pink for Sharpay). Apply the dark shade along your lash line, the medium shade on the crease, and a light shade up to the eyebrow bone but not beyond. Soften and blend any hard edges so one colour seems to melt into the next.

★ To open up your eyes so that they appear livelier, place a dot of a light shadow in the inner corner of each eye.

★ Finish with a coat of mascara – starting at the base of the lashes and giving an even coat to the tips.

★ Add a long sweep of blusher to your cheeks starting from the apples of your cheeks and working backwards to your ears.

★ And finish off your teen star look with a coating of lip gloss! Perfect – you're ready to wow!

Curtain's up!

Sharpay's running late and needs to be on stage in five minutes! Can you help her?

TIP: If you don't know where to put your blusher bend over for 30 seconds, then slowly stand up. Where your cheeks are flushed is where you are meant to blush. Apply your blush there and it will be naturally rosy every time!

TIP: When choosing the perfect eyeshadow shop for shades that complement your skin tone. You want colours that softly contrast with the shade of your eyes - not match them exactly. Ash has brown eyes so she looks gorgeous with bronze, soft pink, brown. But if she wants a more funky look tangerine orange, royal blue, hot pink and lime green also look great!

TIP: Bear in mind that dark colours will minimize your eyes, while light shades will make them stand out.

TIP: Always have some cotton wool and makeup remover to hand – remember even teen stars need to practise!

the show must go on!

Off the back of *High School Musical's* phenomenal success, wheels were put in motion to create a sequel. Of course Ashley signed on immediately, as did the rest of the cast. So, all the gang re-grouped in January 2007. Thing's were a lot easier second time around and it was like a reunion with all the pals back filming together. So much fun!

The second movie is based around the gang's summer vacation. Troy again is in turmoil and has to learn vital life lessons. Presented with an opportunity to sell out his friends to guarantee a scholarship to college, Troy has to make the decision between his pals and his goals, which isn't made easier by the fact that Sharpay has designs on Troy, and is cont-inually plotting to win his heart.

Amazingly the sequel was an even bigger hit than the first! The first broadcast on 17 August 2007

broke all the records, receiving 17.2 million viewers. By the end of the first weekend 33 million viewers had tuned in, making it the most-watched made-for-cable movie ever!

But that wasn't all of it. In 2008 the gang reunited again for *HSM 3: Senior Year*. This time around the Wildcats and company are facing their final year, and with that comes the prom, graduation and of course moving on from East High! Could it be that there'll be no more *High School Musical* films from Ashley, Vanessa and Zac? It looks as if that's the case, sniff. 'It's sad,' says Ashley. 'It feels like we're graduating from *High School*

Musical.' This time the film was released on the big screen. Opening weekend saw queues run around the block outside cinemas across the globe, and the film was a global box office smash!

While it looks like there will be a *High School Musical 4* from Disney, Ashley says the main cast definitely won't be involved next time around. 'We're all doing other projects and moving on,' she says. You never know, though, Hollywood is a funny place where stars have been known to change their mind before, but for the time being East High, Class of 2008 have left the building…

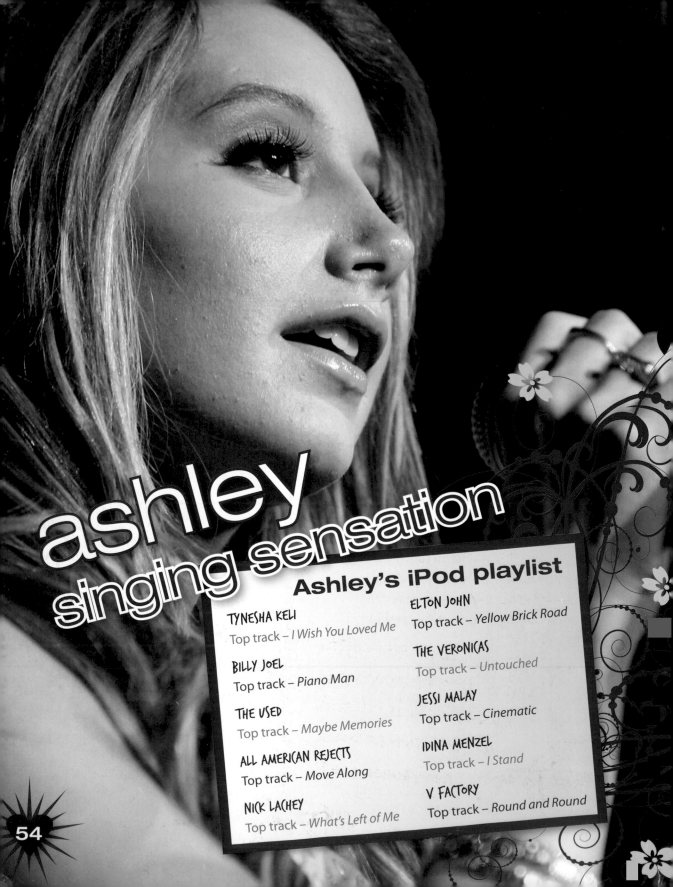

ashley
singing sensation

Ashley's iPod playlist

TYNESHA KELI
Top track – *I Wish You Loved Me*

BILLY JOEL
Top track – *Piano Man*

THE USED
Top track – *Maybe Memories*

ALL AMERICAN REJECTS
Top track – *Move Along*

NICK LACHEY
Top track – *What's Left of Me*

ELTON JOHN
Top track – *Yellow Brick Road*

THE VERONICAS
Top track – *Untouched*

JESSI MALAY
Top track – *Cinematic*

IDINA MENZEL
Top track – *I Stand*

V FACTORY
Top track – *Round and Round*

*E*ver since stepping out and belting out Broadway classics as a keen young star, music has been in Ashley's bones. Through *HSM*, she reached the top of the charts with songs like 'What I've Been Looking For' and 'Bop to the Top'. But chart success was a strange feeling for Ashley: 'I have to say, the weirdest thing was looking at the Billboard charts and seeing, like, Beyoncé and Sean Paul and all these people and then seeing Ashley Tisdale,' says Ash. 'I was, like, "no way!" That was the weirdest thing ever. It was really cool, it was a dream come true.'

Ashley, being the ever-ambitious girl that she is, didn't want to stop with the HSM success, no way! She wanted her own solo career. Sure enough, in early 2007, Ashley released her first solo album, *Headstrong*, which shot to the top of the charts. Suffice to say Ashley's over the moon with her budding musical career: ' It was a dream come true because I really wanted to record and do an album one day.' No doubt plenty more chart hits will be coming from this bright young star in the future!

'I love Ashley's voice, it's so powerful but lovely and soft at the same time.'

Kerry Jones, age 11

ashley today

In no time at all, Ashley has become one of the most well-known teens in the world. But has that changed Ashley? 'Of course not,' she says. 'The fame thing is crazy. My friends around me never let me get carried away. I try not to take too much notice of it all. I just want to keep doing the best job I can for my fans, whom I love.' There's certainly no hope of Ashley going down the crazy wild child path that many child stars have gone down before her. 'My family keep me grounded. I don't drink or do drugs. I don't let those distractions get in the way of my life or my career.'

No diva here!

But surely she must be prone to the odd diva tantrum now she's a chart-topping, big screen, Hollywood name? Not a chance says Ash: 'I'm still me. I think I'll always be grounded because my parents keep me that way. My mom would smack me if I ever started acting like a diva.' Despite all the fame and plaudits, Ashley still likes to keep her feet on the ground and it's this humble, girl-next-door attitude that has won over so many fans.

Kissing & crushing

Ashley is super-private about her lovelife and is keen to keep that part of her life to herself. Despite staying quiet when asked about her relationship with Jared Murillo, she was eventually forced into admitting they were an item after being snapped by the paparazzi more than a few times. 'We're constantly being followed by the paparazzi,' Ashley says. 'I feel bad because he has to deal with it.' Having met on the set of *High School Musical*, where Jared was a backing dancer, the couple have embarked on a serious relationship, and now Zanessa can go on double dates with Jashley. Sweet!

Zashley?

Because of Zac and Ashley's close friendship, rumours have also gone around about a romance between Zac and Ashley – not true, of course. According to Zac the fake story of him and Ashley 'is funny, me and Ashley are good friends. We just laugh every time we hear it. She's very cool and we hang out all the time, but we're definitely not dating.' In reality they're just best buds and regularly go to each other for advice on the opposite sex.

'Ashley's
so talented,
she can do
anything,
and she's
beautiful.'

Lilly Smith, age 12

looking ahead

The future's bright

Seeing how much she's achieved to date in her career, you can bet Ashley's got plenty in store for the future. Immediately after shooting *HSM 3*, Ashley went straight into the recording studio to begin work on her second album 'Autumn Goodbye'. Now that Disney projects *Suite Life* and *HSM* are behind her, can we expect to see a more mature Ashley? Well, it looks like she'll be around the teen genre for a little while to come; she's not got any wrinkles yet! She has a leading role in *Picture This*, a high school rom-com that's due out this year. Naturally, acting as a lead role in the film wasn't enough: she also recorded a song on the soundtrack and was the executive producer of the film! Producing is something she's thrown herself into and something she looks set to do more of. Also due out this year is the adventure comedy, *They Came From Upstairs*, a film about a bunch of teenagers trying to keep aliens out of their holiday home. Sounds spooky!

Now that she's an established Hollywood actress, it looks like her TV days could be over and it's red carpets all the way for Ash!

Picture Credits

Getty: front cover, 2, 8, 9 (right), 12 (top), 13, 14, 16, 17 (right), 23, 35, 36 (bottom), 38, 29 (top), 40 (top), 41 (top), 41 (right), 42, 45, 51, 56, 57, 58, 59, back cover

Rex: 7, 17 (left), 20, 24, 25, 26, 27 (right), 28, 30, 31, 32, 33, 34, 40 (bottom), 43 (top), 44, 47, 49, 52, 53, 54, 55, 63, back cover (bottom left)

PA Photos: 3, 4, 5, 6, 9 (left), 12 (bottom), 21, 22, 29 (right), 26 (top), 37, 46 (left), 61, back cover (top left)

iStock: 3, 9 (bottom), 10, 18 (top & middle), 19, 22 (bottom), 27 (left), 29 (left), 37 (left), 39 (bottom), 41 (left), 42, 43 (bottom), 46 (right), 48, 49 (right), 50, 51 (bottom), 52

Corbis: 11, 60

Alamy: 18 (bottom)

Acknowledgements

Posy Edwards would like to thank Guyan Mitra, Amanda Harris, Helen Ewing, Jane Sturrock, Daniel Bunyard, Briony Hartley, and Rich Carr.

First published in hardback in
Great Britain in 2009 by
Orion Books an imprint of the
Orion Publishing Group Ltd
Orion House, 5 Upper St Martin's Lane, London WC2H 9EA
An Hachette Livre UK Company

10 9 8 7 6 5 4 3 2 1

A CIP catalogue record for this book is available from the British Library.

ISBN: 978 1 4091 0468 1

Designed by Goldust Design
Printed in Spain by Cayfosa

The Orion Publishing Group's policy is to use papers that are natural, renewable and recyclable and made from wood grown in sustainable forests. The logging and manufacturing processes are expected to conform to the environmental regulations of the country of origin.

Every effort has been made to fulfil requirements with regard to reproducing copyright material. The author and publisher will be glad to rectify any omissions at the earliest opportunity.

www.orionbooks.co.uk